EXPANAGRAMS

Exciting Expanding Word Puzzles

JESSE LEONG

iUniverse, Inc.
Bloomington

Expanagrams
Exciting Expanding Word Puzzles

iUniverse books may be ordered through booksellers or by contacting:

iUniverse
1663 Liberty Drive
Bloomington, IN 47403
www.iuniverse.com
1-800-Authors (1-800-288-4677)

ISBN: 978-1-4620-1639-6 (pbk)
ISBN: 978-1-4620-1640-2 (ebk)

Printed in the United States of America

iUniverse rev. date: 07/18/2011

To my beloved Mom and Dad, who bought us encyclopedias and a big dictionary when we were children, and to my dear brothers Al, Bayne, and Vince, and my dear friend, Bob, all puzzle masters.

Contents

I.   INTRODUCTION

Welcome to *Expanagrams*! The Expanagram is an exciting and aesthetically pleasing word puzzle quite unlike any other! It's a unique concept of my own creation, one that I invented for your enjoyment. The concept is easy to learn and the puzzles are fun and challenging to solve. As its name suggest, an Expanagram is a sort of expanding anagram. Basically, you as the solver add a specified letter to a given word, rearrange the letters to form a new word, and then you keep adding specific letters, which may occasionally be hidden, to form a unique series of progressively lengthier, expanding words.

As mentioned, the Expanagram is a distinctive concept. Unlike scramble puzzles where one makes a coherent word out of an incoherent batch of letters, an Expanagram requires you to make a coherent word out of another coherent word and an additional letter. As well, solving an Expanagram is not precisely like solving a straight anagram because of that additional letter. And again, that additional letter may occasionally be hidden, which underscores the uniqueness. These features plus, of course, its expanding nature make the Expanagram a unique concept and puzzle.

While this overall concept is easy to grasp, the actual Expanagram puzzles may not always be as easy. But they're always fun and I would encourage you to keep plugging away, even, especially, when they're stumpers. This is because you never know what untapped ability you may find inside yourself until you're put to the test! Speaking of plugging away, I would ask you to do this even when a few puzzles seem reminiscent of ones you previously did in the book. As with snowflakes, no two puzzles in the book are exactly alike, and while a few may begin or progress similarly, none conclude the same way.

As trial and error may be necessary for any puzzle, I would go on to suggest getting a pencil to do the puzzles, especially if you prefer not to mark up the book permanently. Should you wish not to mark up the book at all, you could just write out the answers on another sheet of paper. Another strong reason for keeping the book unblemished is that this would allow you to revisit these puzzles afresh, plus the accompanying text, weeks, months, half a decade, or at any point later, even the puzzles you've already solved. You'd be surprised how tricky certain puzzle solutions are to remember only weeks later, let alone months or more later. I speak from experience. There were a few occasions when I created puzzles without writing down their solutions right away, and later on, I actually had to solve my own puzzles! It was astounding to be stumped momentarily by puzzles that I myself had created!

Please be sure to read the Instructions and Rules, which immediately follow this introduction. Then check out the Warm-up section to get a feel for the puzzles. The 140 Expanagram puzzles are grouped mainly by letter length, with the briefest puzzle being a five-letter Expanagram and the lengthiest a 10-letter Expanagram. The puzzles are arranged in the book from briefest to lengthiest, from the relatively straight-forward to the more challenging. The beginning letter for the puzzle word answers will run the gamut almost literally from A to Z, though the words and puzzles won't be presented in alphabetical order, and these word answers will be frequently colorful and descriptive.

As well, check out the Expanagram Exclusives, which are quite distinct from the other puzzles because with these, all the word answers will be exclusive to a certain category for each puzzle (e.g. Animal and Insect Kingdom). These Expanagram Exclusives are sandwiched between the six-letter Expanagrams and seven-letter Expanagrams sections because these categorized puzzles are of those letter lengths.

All the Expanagram puzzles will appear on a page on the right-hand side. The solutions corresponding to the puzzles on a given page will be on the back of that page. This configuration was chosen to allow you quick and easy access to the solutions without having to flip continually to the back of the book and rummage there to find them. But in any case, be sure not to let your roving eye catch a glimpse of solutions to other puzzles while checking on the solution you do want to see! One big suggestion is to do one whole page of puzzles at a stretch prior to turning the page over to see the solutions corresponding to that page.

Obviously, it's your choice as to which sequence you follow in approaching the puzzles. But following the order of the book is not a bad idea because that way, you could match your wits in gradual proportion to the increasing length and complexity of the puzzles, monitor your progress, build momentum, and go from strength to strength. You may well begin to see words more clearly, discerning their configurations, their interrelationships, their magic! Another reason for following the book sequence is that there will be running commentary and the references will be largely cumulative.

I have been a lifelong wordsmith, but while creating these puzzles, I found I was still unearthing eye-opening subtleties about words. As an example, I was thinking about the word "slide" and my first impression was that I wouldn't be able to utilize all its letters to make another word, i.e. an anagram. But not only did I find an anagram; I found three! Relatively speaking, none of these anagrams struck me as being obvious to find, yet they're all valid, recognizable words. First, I realized "delis" was lurking quietly there. Then later, on an unrelated tangent, I happened to be thinking about the word "sidle" and realized with surprise that this, too, was a subtle anagram. The letter configuration of "sidle" led me to see that "idles" was yet one more. The same thing occurred with the word "decimal"; I found three anagrams when I expected to find none, particularly as this was a lengthier word. First, I saw "claimed" which led me to "declaim", and then weeks later, I was surprised to find "medical"!

I want to mention one final example, which has a seasonal touch. I was thinking about the word "silent", and as with the others, unexpectedly I found three anagrams. First, I saw "listen" which quickly led me to see "enlist". Then as Christmas approached, I found one appropriate for the holidays: "tinsel"! Christmas then brought me back to the original word "silent", which now reminded me of "Silent Night". Suddenly, I realized that "night", a word which obviously I first learned as a kid, held an anagram all along: "thing". Hence, "Silent Night" was doing the "tinsel thing", a seemingly appropriate anagram! These examples along with others involving the dynamics of my own Expanagram concept led to a virtual axiom for me: just when you think you can't make a word out of a combination of letters, that's when you just may! This may be something to keep in mind when approaching the Expanagram puzzles.

Creating the Expanagram puzzles was a wondrous, rewarding experience that provided me with continual joy and a number of transcendent, epiphanous moments. I saw words in a fresh way, in a sense, with a different sort of clarity, frequently creating words and puzzles out of what appeared to be impossibly difficult groups of letters. It's enthralling to create an aesthetically pleasing thing, and it's fulfilling to apply oneself to a thing one loves—in my case, the very act of creating.

I hope, then, that you experience a similar exhilaration when you solve any of these puzzles, especially the ones that challenged you the most and that you didn't think you'd be able to untangle. It's uplifting when you face a puzzle that, at first, seems insoluble but by remaining positive and persistent, you solve the thing. And don't be surprised to find that by applying this same systematic, persistent approach, you may well solve other things in life and reach your goals.

Generally, I hope you have as much fun and find as much enlightenment in solving these Expanagram puzzles as I did in creating them. I hope the *Expanagrams* book and puzzles help you discover or rediscover the beauty, joy, and magic of words. Many thanks for your interest. Take care and have fun!

Jesse Leong

EXPANAGRAMS Exciting Expanding Word Puzzles! Expand Your Vocabulary! From GO-BRAINERS BOOKS. "XLR8 your brain and accelerate your fun, too!"

II.   INSTRUCTIONS AND RULES

1. Take the given word on the first line and add the new letter indicated on that line and rearrange all these letters to form a new word. Print your word answer on the next line in the blanks provided. Then add the next new letter indicated on that line to your word answer and rearrange all those letters to form another new word, and print that word answer on the next line. Keep repeating these steps, forming progressively lengthier words on each line, down to the last line. Occasionally, a new letter to be added will not be given; it'll be a blank representing a hidden letter which you must figure out yourself. The right combination of expanding word answers represents the unique, overall solution.

2. Words must be found in a English dictionary. Not allowable as word answers are:
- initials (e.g. NCAA)
- contractions (e.g. don't, 'twas)
- possessives requiring an apostrophe (children's)
- abbreviations requiring a period (e.g. dept.), which means that abbreviations not requiring a period are allowable (e.g. umps)
- interjections (e.g. "whoa", "ouch")
- words or names that are always capitalized (e.g. Chad, Guam)

3. Hyphenated words are allowable. As well, the only foreign words allowable are those found in an English dictionary, and these are generally recognizable (e.g. taco, haiku).

4. Words pluralized or formed with "s" or "es" at the end of a root word and words put into the past tense with "d" or "ed" are allowable provided the root word and the lengthened word meet all the other rules, especially the next rule.

5. Your overall solution to each puzzle cannot have any words followed immediately on the next line by the same word with an "s" or "d" added to the end of that word (and this rule applies to the given word on the first line as well). As an example, the word answer "fine" cannot be followed immediately on the next line by "fines" or "fined". You must choose some combination of word answers to generate such an overall solution.

As an additional example, if your word answer on a line was "feat" and the next new letter to be added was "s", you couldn't choose "feats" as your word answer on the next line. You must, in accordance with this rule, choose another word answer such as "feast". Or you could change your word answer on that first line to "fate", and now you could choose "feats" as your word answer on the next line. Either of these combinations would meet this rule. Occasionally, there may be only one possible word combination to meet this rule.

6. Words spelled in American English and words spelled in the King's English, utilized, for example, in the United Kingdom and Canada, are equally allowable (e.g. American English: rigor, jewelry; King's English: rigour, jewellery).

7. The word answer on each line must be a single word combining all the necessary letters, not multiple words combining all the necessary letters.

8. Occasionally, there may be more than one possible answer on a line. Overall, though, there will be a unique solution for each puzzle.

III. WARM-UP

#1
1. BET + D
2. _ _ _ _ + U
3. _ _ _ _ _

#2
1. ALE + C
2. _ _ _ _ + D
3. _ _ _ _ _

#3
1. CUP + S
2. _ _ _ _ + K
3. _ _ _ _ _

#4 Here's a first taste of the hidden letter puzzles. Again, that's where a new letter to be added will not be given; it'll be a blank representing that hidden letter which you must figure out yourself.

1. HUT + R
2. _ _ _ _ + _
3. _ _ _ _ _

SOLUTIONS:

#1
1. BET + D
2. DEBT
3. DEBUT*

*Hope you made a promising DEBUT!

#2
1. ALE + C
2. LACE
3. DECAL*

*DECAL is the necessary word answer on line 3. Remember, you can't choose LACED as your word answer on line 3 based on Rule 5 from the Instructions and Rules.

#3
1. CUP + S
2. CUSP*
3. PUCKS

*CUSP is the necessary word answer on line 2. Again, you can't choose CUPS as your word answer on line 2 based once more on Rule 5, which applies to the given word on the first line as well.

By the way, can you tell I'm a hockey fan? To my way of thinking, if the Toronto Leafs filled the net with lot more PUCKS, they'd be on the CUSP of finally winning the Stanley Cup! And speaking of sports, you'll see a sports-related puzzle in the Expanagram Exclusives and a secret baseball-related page later in the book!

#4
1. HUT + R
2. HURT Hidden letter is: T
3. TRUTH

Now that you're warmed up, give the rest of the puzzles a go. Keep enjoying!

IV.   5-LETTER EXPANAGRAMS

#5
1. BAG + N
2. _ _ _ _ + E
3. _ _ _ _ _

#6
1. OAR + D
2. _ _ _ _ + I
3. _ _ _ _ _

#7
1. ILK + C
2. _ _ _ _ + S
3. _ _ _ _ _

#8
1. OUR + H
2. _ _ _ _ + _
3. _ _ _ _ _

SOLUTIONS:

#5
1. BAG* + N
2. BANG*
3. BEGAN*

*Hope you BEGAN with a BANG and the rest is in the BAG!

#6
1. OAR + D
2. ROAD
3. RADIO

#7
1. ILK + C
2. LICK
3. SLICK

#8
1. OUR + H
2. HOUR Hidden letter is: M
3. HUMOR

#9
1. CUE + L
2. _ _ _ _ + N
3. _ _ _ _ _

#10
1. IRE + P
2. _ _ _ _ + V
3. _ _ _ _ _

#11
1. PRY + S
2. _ _ _ _ + U
3. _ _ _ _ _

#12
1. GUM + L
2. _ _ _ _ + _
3. _ _ _ _ _

SOLUTIONS:

#9
1. CUE + L
2. CLUE
3. UNCLE

#10
1. IRE + P
2. PIER or RIPE
3. VIPER

#11
1. PRY + S
2. SPRY
3. SYRUP

#12
1. GUM* + L
2. GLUM Hidden letter is: O
3. MOGUL

*GUM, MUG. Here's a curious pair of anagrams which both refer to parts of the body. The given word, GUM, refers obviously to the teeth while its anagram, MUG, is an informal term for "face". Can you think of another pair of anagrams which both refer to body parts? No? Hang on, you'll see another pair like that later!

V.   6-LETTER EXPANAGRAMS

#13
1. OLE + V
2. _ _ _ _ + S
3. _ _ _ _ _ + W
4. _ _ _ _ _ _

#14
1. TEE + R
2. _ _ _ _ + N
3. _ _ _ _ _ + L
4. _ _ _ _ _ _

#15
1. FIN + E
2. _ _ _ _ + D
3. _ _ _ _ _ + R
4. _ _ _ _ _ _

SOLUTIONS:

#13

1. OLE + V
2. LOVE*
3. SOLVE*
4. VOWELS* or WOLVES

*This book celebrates the beauty and joy of words and hence, includes positive words that are special to me and most of us such as TRUTH, HUMOR, and others. And there could be no word that's more important to me personally than the six-letter word highlighting the last puzzle of this section. With this in mind, we had to begin this section with a puzzle highlighting the word that conquers all: LOVE! And specifically relating to this book, *Expanagrams* is for people who LOVE to SOLVE puzzles with consonants and VOWELS!

#14

1. TEE + R
2. TREE
3. ENTER
4. RELENT

#15

1. FIN + E
2. FINE
3. FIEND
4. FRIEND*

*If you have difficulty remembering whether FRIEND is spelled with "ie" or "ei", just remember the spelling with a tip I learned from Mr. Bennett, my fine teacher from grade school: when you're at school or on the job, FRI(day) is the END of the week!

#16
1. AIR + A
2. _ _ _ _ + T
3. _ _ _ _ _ + L
4. _ _ _ _ _ _

#17
1. HOE + C
2. _ _ _ _ + R
3. _ _ _ _ _ + I
4. _ _ _ _ _ _

#18
1. RUE + C
2. _ _ _ _ + L
3. _ _ _ _ _ + D
4. _ _ _ _ _ _

#19
1. SUM + L
2. _ _ _ _ + A
3. _ _ _ _ _ + Q
4. _ _ _ _ _ _

#20
1. UPS + L
2. _ _ _ _ + _
3. _ _ _ _ _ + P
4. _ _ _ _ _ _

SOLUTIONS:

#16
1. AIR + A
2. ARIA
3. TIARA or ATRIA*
4. LARIAT

*ATRIA is the plural for ATRIUM which is a skylit central area in a building or a heart cavity.

#17
1. HOE + C
2. ECHO
3. CHORE or OCHRE
4. HEROIC

#18
1. RUE + C
2. CURE or ECRU
3. ULCER* or CRUEL*
4. CURLED

*ULCER, CRUEL. Here's a curious example of a pair of anagrams which seem appropriate for each other! Ouch! Hence, try not to worry over inconsequential things and just enjoy yourself—with these puzzles, for example!

#19
1. SUM + L
2. SLUM
3. MAULS
4. QUALMS

#20
1. UPS + L
2. PLUS Hidden letter is: E
3. PULSE
4. SUPPLE

#21 (To Elaine)
1. OWL + B
2. _ _ _ _ + E
3. _ _ _ _ _ + R
4. _ _ _ _ _ _

#22
1. HAS + L
2. _ _ _ _ + U
3. _ _ _ _ _ + G
4. _ _ _ _ _ _

#23
1. AXE + L
2. _ _ _ _ + S
3. _ _ _ _ _ + T
4. _ _ _ _ _ _

#24
1. RUN + B
2. _ _ _ _ + _
3. _ _ _ _ _ + E
4. _ _ _ _ _ _

SOLUTIONS:

#21
1. OWL + B
2. BOWL or BLOW
3. ELBOW* or BOWEL*
4. BOWLER

*ELBOW, BOWEL. Here's the other pair of anagrams which both refer to body parts!

#22
1. HAS + L
2. LASH
3. HAULS
4. LAUGHS*

*It's appropriate to follow up a puzzle that mentioned ELBOW with a puzzle that mentions LAUGHS because we all know where the funny bone is positioned!

#23
1. AXE + L
2. AXLE
3. LAXES
4. EXALTS

#24
1. RUN + B
2. BURN Hidden letter is: A
3. URBAN*
4. URBANE*

*URBAN is related to the city and is the opposite of "rural". URBANE is to be refined or suave.

#25

    1. WAS + N

    2. _ _ _ _ + R

    3. _ _ _ _ _ + E

    4. _ _ _ _ _ _

#26 (To James)

    1. OAR + S

    2. _ _ _ _ + N

    3. _ _ _ _ _ + P

    4. _ _ _ _ _ _

#27

    1. EAR + Z

    2. _ _ _ _ + B

    3. _ _ _ _ _ + N

    4. _ _ _ _ _ _

#28

    1. RUB + L

    2. _ _ _ _ + _

    3. _ _ _ _ _ + R

    4. _ _ _ _ _ _

SOLUTIONS:

#25
1. WAS + N
2. SWAN
3. WARNS
4. ANSWER

#26
1. OAR + S
2. SOAR
3. SONAR
4. APRONS

#27
1. EAR + Z
2. RAZE
3. ZEBRA
4. BRAZEN

#28
1. RUB + L
2. BLUR Hidden letter is: Y
3. BURLY
4. BLURRY

#29

1. TAG + N
2. _ _ _ _ + U
3. _ _ _ _ _ + O
4. _ _ _ _ _ _

#30

1. BUT + A
2. _ _ _ _ + L
3. _ _ _ _ _ + R
4. _ _ _ _ _ _

#31

1. ALL+ M
2. _ _ _ _ + S
3. _ _ _ _ _ + O
4. _ _ _ _ _ _

#32

1. ONE + _
2. _ _ _ _ + O
3. _ _ _ _ _ + S
4. _ _ _ _ _ _

SOLUTIONS:

#29
1. TAG + N
2. GNAT
3. GAUNT
4. NOUGAT

#30
1. BUT + A
2. TUBA
3. TUBAL
4. BRUTAL

#31
1. ALL+ M
2. MALL
3. SMALL
4. SLALOM

#32
1. ONE + _ Hidden letter is: Z
2. ZONE
3. OZONE
4. SNOOZE

#33

    1. OAR + B

    2. _ _ _ _ + H

    3. _ _ _ _ _ + R

    4. _ _ _ _ _ _

#34

    1. AIR + N

    2. _ _ _ _ + D

    3. _ _ _ _ _ + C

    4. _ _ _ _ _ _

#35

    1. ICE + N

    2. _ _ _ _ + H

    3. _ _ _ _ _ + R

    4. _ _ _ _ _ _

#36

    1. ROE + H

    2. _ _ _ _ + T

    3. _ _ _ _ _ + M

    4. _ _ _ _ _ _

SOLUTIONS:

#33
    1. OAR + B
    2. BOAR
    3. ABHOR
    4. HARBOR

#34
    1. AIR + N
    2. RAIN
    3. DRAIN
    4. RANCID

#35
    1. ICE + N
    2. NICE
    3. NICHE
    4. ENRICH

#36
    1. ROE* + H
    2. HERO*
    3. OTHER
    4. MOTHER*

*MOTHER, HERO. It's entirely appropriate to find the word HERO in the word MOTHER because of a mother's unconditional love and the sacrifices she makes for her children. This is how I feel about mothers, generally. And naturally, it's how I especially feel about my own mother! And the word that I mentioned previously that was the most important to me personally, well…Mum's the word!

By the way, ROE is a small deer. And ROEBUCK (like that department store) is a male deer, which means that ROE on its own could refer to a female or mother deer—or that should be Mother, *dear*!

VI.   EXPANAGRAM EXCLUSIVES

Unlike the other puzzles, these Expanagram Exclusives puzzles all have word answers that are exclusive to a certain category for each puzzle. Where there's more than one possible answer on a particular line, please choose only the word answers that are related to the category in question.

Animal and Insect Kingdom
This will be the category for the next four puzzles, and with this category, the word answer on each line will be creatures from the animal and insect kingdom.

#37
   1. SAG + T
   2. _ _ _ _ + O
   3. _ _ _ _ _ + R
   4. _ _ _ _ _ _

#38
   1. SUM + E
   2. _ _ _ _ + L
   3. _ _ _ _ _ + S
   4. _ _ _ _ _ _

#39
   1. ABS + O
   2. _ _ _ _ + R
   3. _ _ _ _ _ + C
   4. _ _ _ _ _ _

#40
   1. ORE + S
   2. _ _ _ _ + H
   3. _ _ _ _ _ + N
   4. _ _ _ _ _ _ + T
   5. _ _ _ _ _ _ _

SOLUTIONS:

#37

1. SAG + T
2. STAG
3. GOATS
4. GATORS

#38

1. SUM + E
2. EMUS
3. MULES
4. MUSSEL

#39

1. ABS + O
2. BOAS
3. BOARS
4. COBRAS

#40

1. ORE + S
2. ROES
3. HORSE
4. HERONS
5. HORNETS

Theatrical Arts

The word answer on each line will be things and specific productions related to the theatrical arts. And for this puzzle only, capitalized words will be allowable—for the name of a musical and an opera.

#41
1. SAC + T
2. _ _ _ _ + O (one possible answer on this line is the name of a musical)
3. _ _ _ _ _ + R (the answer on this line is the name of an opera)
4. _ _ _ _ _ _

Sports and Recreation

The word answer on each line will be things and activities related to sports and recreation.

#42
1. IRE + D
2. _ _ _ _ + V
3. _ _ _ _ _ + R
4. _ _ _ _ _ _

Fruits and Vegetables

The word answer on each line will be specific fruits or vegetables.

#43
1. SAP + E
2. _ _ _ _ + R
3. _ _ _ _ _ + G
4. _ _ _ _ _ _

Food

The word answer on each line will be things and ideas related to food.

#44
1. SIP + E
2. _ _ _ _ + C
3. _ _ _ _ _ + R
4. _ _ _ _ _ _ + E
5. _ _ _ _ _ _

SOLUTIONS:

#41
1. SAC + T
2. ACTS or CAST or *CATS*
3. *TOSCA*
4. ACTORS or CO-STAR

#42
1. IRE + D
2. RIDE*
3. DIVER or DRIVE**
4. DRIVER***

*RIDE refers to equestrian sports.
**DIVER refers to pool diving or skydiving while DRIVE refers to auto racing or golf.
***DRIVER refers to golf equipment or auto racing.

#43
1. SAP + E
2. PEAS
3. PEARS
4. GRAPES

#44
1. SIP + E
2. PIES
3. SPICE
4. PRICES
5. RECIPES

VII. 7-LETTER EXPANAGRAMS

#45
1. GEM + A
2. _ _ _ _ + I
3. _ _ _ _ _ + R
4. _ _ _ _ _ _ + C
5. _ _ _ _ _ _

#46
1. PET + O
2. _ _ _ _ + D
3. _ _ _ _ _ + R
4. _ _ _ _ _ _ + O
5. _ _ _ _ _ _

#47
1. SEE + N
2. _ _ _ _ + C
3. _ _ _ _ _ + I
4. _ _ _ _ _ _ + C
5. _ _ _ _ _ _

#48 (To these athletes: Mary, Raymond, Jen, Jeff, and Joanna. And to another athlete, Jackie D.)
1. ROE + S
2. _ _ _ _ + C
3. _ _ _ _ _ + C
4. _ _ _ _ _ _ + E
5. _ _ _ _ _ _

SOLUTIONS:

#45
1. GEM + A
2. GAME
3. IMAGE
4. MIRAGE or IMAGER
5. GRIMACE

#46
1. PET + O
2. POET
3. DEPOT
4. DEPORT
5. TORPEDO

#47
1. SEE + N
2. SEEN
3. SCENE
4. NIECES
5. SCIENCE

#48
1. ROE+ S
2. SORE or ROSE
3. SCORE or CORES
4. SOCCER
5. COERCES

#49

1. ROT + N
2. _ _ _ _ + E
3. _ _ _ _ _ + M
4. _ _ _ _ _ _ + T
5. _ _ _ _ _ _

#50

1. NOR + C
2. _ _ _ _ + A
3. _ _ _ _ _ + Y
4. _ _ _ _ _ _ + M
5. _ _ _ _ _ _

#51

1. ERE + T
2. _ _ _ _ + D
3. _ _ _ _ _ + I
4. _ _ _ _ _ _ + U
5. _ _ _ _ _ _

#52

1. RIG + T
2. _ _ _ _ + S
3. _ _ _ _ _ + E
4. _ _ _ _ _ _ + S
5. _ _ _ _ _ _

SOLUTIONS:

#49
1. ROT + N
2. TORN
3. TENOR or TONER
4. MENTOR
5. TORMENT

#50
1. NOR + C
2. CORN
3. ACORN
4. CRAYON
5. ACRONYM

#51
1. ERE + T
2. TREE
3. DETER
4. DIETER
5. ERUDITE

#52
1. RIG + T
2. GRIT or TRIG
3. GRIST or GRITS
4. TIGERS
5. TIGRESS

#53 (To Deana)
1. GIN + S
2. _ _ _ _ + L
3. _ _ _ _ _ + O
4. _ _ _ _ _ _ + B
5. _ _ _ _ _ _

#54
1. SIC + E
2. _ _ _ _ + T
3. _ _ _ _ _ + U
4. _ _ _ _ _ _ + J
5. _ _ _ _ _ _

#55
1. EEL + P
2. _ _ _ _ + R
3. _ _ _ _ _ + A
4. _ _ _ _ _ _ + S
5. _ _ _ _ _ _

#56
1. AIL + S
2. _ _ _ _ + A
3. _ _ _ _ _ + S
4. _ _ _ _ _ _ + E
5. _ _ _ _ _ _

SOLUTIONS:

#53
   1. GIN + S
   2. SING or SIGN
   3. SLING
   4. LINGOS
   5. GOBLINS

#54

   1. SIC + E
   2. ICES
   3. CITES
   4. CUTIES
   5. JUSTICE

#55
   1. EEL + P
   2. PEEL
   3. LEPER or REPEL*
   4. REPEAL
   5. RELAPSE or PLEASER

*LEPER, REPEL. Here's another curious example of how certain words seem to have highly appropriate anagrams where the pair of words inform and illustrate each other! LEPER is a person afflicted with leprosy, a contagious disease and hence, needs to be quarantined. REPEL means to drive away, which is the unfortunate but necessary effect a leper's condition would have on other people as it'd be imperative not to have the disease spread.

#56
   1. AIL + S
   2. SAIL
   3. ALIAS
   4. ASSAIL
   5. ALIASES

57

1. LAB + D
2. _ _ _ _ + E
3. _ _ _ _ _ + R
4. _ _ _ _ _ _ + U
5. _ _ _ _ _ _

#58

1. MET + R
2. _ _ _ _ + E
3. _ _ _ _ _ + O
4. _ _ _ _ _ _ + S
5. _ _ _ _ _ _

#59

1. SIT + U
2. _ _ _ _ + E
3. _ _ _ _ _ + D
4. _ _ _ _ _ _ + O
5. _ _ _ _ _ _

#60

1. RAG + C
2. _ _ _ _ + O
3. _ _ _ _ _ + _
4. _ _ _ _ _ _ + E
5. _ _ _ _ _ _

SOLUTIONS:

#57
1. LAB + D
2. BALD
3. BLADE or BALED
4. BLARED
5. DURABLE

#58
1. MET + R
2. TERM
3. METER or METRE
4. REMOTE
5. METEORS

#59
1. SIT + U
2. SUIT
3. SUITE
4. DUTIES
5. OUTSIDE

#60
1. RAG + C
2. CRAG
3. CARGO Hidden letter is: U
4. COUGAR
5. COURAGE

#61
1. LEG + S
2. _ _ _ _ + N
3. _ _ _ _ _ + I
4. _ _ _ _ _ _ + H
5. _ _ _ _ _ _ _

#62
1. LED + B
2. _ _ _ _ + U
3. _ _ _ _ _ + O
4. _ _ _ _ _ _ + R
5. _ _ _ _ _ _ _

#63
1. TIP + R
2. _ _ _ _ + E
3. _ _ _ _ _ + L
4. _ _ _ _ _ _ + E
5. _ _ _ _ _ _ _

#64
1. ORE + M
2. _ _ _ _ + H
3. _ _ _ _ _ + T
4. _ _ _ _ _ _ + E
5. _ _ _ _ _ _ _

SOLUTIONS:

#61
1. LEG + S
2. GELS
3. GLENS
4. SINGLE
5. SHINGLE

#62
1. LED + B
2. BLED
3. LUBED
4. DOUBLE
5. BOULDER

#63
1. TIP + R
2. TRIP
3. TRIPE
4. TRIPLE
5. REPTILE

#64
1. ORE + M
2. MORE
3. HOMER*
4. MOTHER
5. THEOREM

*This is the secret baseball-related page that was mentioned previously! Did you happen to notice the following three words among your word answers in the last three puzzles respectively: SINGLE, DOUBLE, TRIPLE? Hence, this puzzle had to include the next logical word in that sequence: HOMER!

#65
1. NET + R
2. _ _ _ _ + U
3. _ _ _ _ _ + A
4. _ _ _ _ _ _ + L
5. _ _ _ _ _ _ _

#66 (To Todd)
1. IRE + W
2. _ _ _ _ + S
3. _ _ _ _ _ + T
4. _ _ _ _ _ _ + R
5. _ _ _ _ _ _ _

#67
1. ERE + S
2. _ _ _ _ + A
3. _ _ _ _ _ + L
4. _ _ _ _ _ _ + E
5. _ _ _ _ _ _ _

#68
1. BOO + E
2. _ _ _ _ + _
3. _ _ _ _ _ + D
4. _ _ _ _ _ _ + N
5. _ _ _ _ _ _ _

SOLUTIONS:

#65
1. NET + R
2. RENT or TERN
3. TUNER
4. NATURE
5. NEUTRAL

#66
1. IRE + W
2. WIRE
3. WISER
4. WRITES
5. WRITERS

#67
1. ERE + S
2. SEER
3. ERASE
4. RESALE
5. RELEASE

#68
1. BOO + E
2. OBOE Hidden letter is: K
3. EBOOK
4. BOOKED
5. BOOKEND

#69
1. ALE + C
2. _ _ _ _ + R
3. _ _ _ _ _ + O
4. _ _ _ _ _ _ + I
5. _ _ _ _ _ _

#70
1. ONE + C
2. _ _ _ _ + S
3. _ _ _ _ _ + C
4. _ _ _ _ _ _ + I
5. _ _ _ _ _ _

#71
1. LEG + D
2. _ _ _ _ + I
3. _ _ _ _ _ + R
4. _ _ _ _ _ _ + D
5. _ _ _ _ _ _

SOLUTIONS:

#69
1. ALE + C
2. LACE
3. CLEAR
4. ORACLE
5. CALORIE

#70
1. ONE + C
2. CONE or ONCE
3. SCONE or CONES*
4. SCONCE
5. CONCISE

*SCONE, CONES. Here are a pair of anagrams that both refer to food and more specifically, treats! SCONE refers to a biscuit. And if you saw CONES on a menu, that would refer to a treat which most people, especially children, love: ice cream! Can you think of another pair of anagrams that are both the names of foods? Not yet? Well, hold that thought—that food for thought—because you'll see another pair later!

#71
1. LEG + D
2. GELD
3. GLIDE
4. GLIDER or GIRDLE
5. GRIDDLE*

*GRIDDLE is what a SCONE, mentioned in the previous puzzle, would be baked on.

#72
1. OVA + L
2. _ _ _ _ + S
3. _ _ _ _ _ + E
4. _ _ _ _ _ _ + B
5. _ _ _ _ _ _

#73
1. ONE + S
2. _ _ _ _ + S
3. _ _ _ _ _ + I
4. _ _ _ _ _ _ + S
5. _ _ _ _ _ _

#74 (To Gary Ryb.)
1. GIN + S
2. _ _ _ _ + R
3. _ _ _ _ _ + E
4. _ _ _ _ _ _ + O
5. _ _ _ _ _ _

#75
1. LAB + E
2. _ _ _ _ + R
3. _ _ _ _ _ + A
4. _ _ _ _ _ _ + P
5. _ _ _ _ _ _

#76
1. HEM + S
2. _ _ _ _ + _
3. _ _ _ _ _ + D
4. _ _ _ _ _ _ + A
5. _ _ _ _ _ _

SOLUTIONS:

#72
  1. OVA + L
  2. OVAL
  3. SALVO
  4. LOAVES
  5. ABSOLVE

#73
  1. ONE + S
  2. EONS
  3. NOSES
  4. NOISES
  5. SESSION

#74
  1. GIN + S
  2. SING or SIGN
  3. RINGS or GRINS
  4. SINGER or RESIGNS or RE-SIGNS or REIGNS
  5. REGIONS

#75
  1. LAB + E
  2. ABLE or BALE
  3. BLARE or ABLER
  4. ARABLE
  5. PARABLE

#76
  1. HEM + S
  2. MESH Hidden letter is: A
  3. SHAME
  4. MASHED
  5. ASHAMED

#77

  1. TEE + H
  2. _ _ _ _ + T
  3. _ _ _ _ _ + R
  4. _ _ _ _ _ _ + A
  5. _ _ _ _ _ _

#78

  1. ACT + T
  2. _ _ _ _ + I
  3. _ _ _ _ _ + S
  4. _ _ _ _ _ _ + C
  5. _ _ _ _ _ _

#79

  1. RID + N
  2. _ _ _ _ + K
  3. _ _ _ _ _ + E
  4. _ _ _ _ _ _ + D
  5. _ _ _ _ _ _

#80

  1. PET + R
  2. _ _ _ _ + C
  3. _ _ _ _ _ + I
  4. _ _ _ _ _ _ + U
  5. _ _ _ _ _ _

SOLUTIONS:

#77
1. TEE + H
2. THEE
3. TEETH
4. TETHER
5. THEATER

#78
1. ACT + T
2. TACT
3. ATTIC
4. STATIC
5. TACTICS

#79
1. RID + N
2. RIND
3. DRINK
4. KINDER
5. KINDRED

#80
1. PET + R
2. PERT
3. CREPT
4. TRICEP
5. PICTURE

#81
1. ANY + M
2. _ _ _ _ + L
3. _ _ _ _ _ + A
4. _ _ _ _ _ _ + O
5. _ _ _ _ _ _ _

#82 (To Bob)
1. TOP + R
2. _ _ _ _ + E
3. _ _ _ _ _ + Y
4. _ _ _ _ _ _ + T
5. _ _ _ _ _ _ _

#83
1. ONE + S
2. _ _ _ _ + D
3. _ _ _ _ _ + R
4. _ _ _ _ _ _ + V
5. _ _ _ _ _ _ _

#84
1. LED + B
2. _ _ _ _ + A
3. _ _ _ _ _ + _
4. _ _ _ _ _ _ + L
5. _ _ _ _ _ _ _

SOLUTIONS:

#81
1. ANY + M
2. MANY
3. MANLY
4. LAYMAN
5. ANOMALY

#82
1. TOP + R
2. PORT
3. TROPE
4. POETRY
5. POTTERY

#83
1. ONE + S
2. NOSE or EONS
3. NODES or NOSED
4. SNORED or DRONES*
5. VENDORS

*SNORED, DRONES. Here's another example, an amusing one, of a pair of anagrams which seem appropriate for each other!

#84
1. LED + B
2. BLED
3. BLADE Hidden letter is: E
4. BEADLE
5. LABELED

#85
1. RUE + T
2. _ _ _ _ + T
3. _ _ _ _ _ + B
4. _ _ _ _ _ _ + I
5. _ _ _ _ _ _ _

#86
1. SEA + E
2. _ _ _ _ + R
3. _ _ _ _ _ + C
4. _ _ _ _ _ _ + T
5. _ _ _ _ _ _ _

#87
1. TEA + N
2. _ _ _ _ + M
3. _ _ _ _ _ + D
4. _ _ _ _ _ _ + A
5. _ _ _ _ _ _ _

#88
1. DAY + R
2. _ _ _ _ + E
3. _ _ _ _ _ + F
4. _ _ _ _ _ _ + S
5. _ _ _ _ _ _ _

SOLUTIONS:

#85
1. RUE + T
2. TRUE
3. UTTER
4. BUTTER
5. TRIBUTE

#86
1. SEA + E
2. EASE
3. ERASE
4. CREASE
5. CREATES

#87
1. TEA + N
2. NEAT or ANTE
3. MEANT
4. TANDEM
5. MANDATE

#88
1. DAY + R
2. YARD
3. READY
4. FRAYED
5. DEFRAYS

#89
1. RED + I
2. _ _ _ _ + D
3. _ _ _ _ _ + B
4. _ _ _ _ _ _ + A
5. _ _ _ _ _ _

#90
1. FAN + L
2. _ _ _ _ + I
3. _ _ _ _ _ + E
4. _ _ _ _ _ _ + G
5. _ _ _ _ _ _

#91
1. ICE + L
2. _ _ _ _ + S
3. _ _ _ _ _ + P
4. _ _ _ _ _ _ + A
5. _ _ _ _ _ _

#92
1. RUE + N
2. _ _ _ _ + R
3. _ _ _ _ _ + T
4. _ _ _ _ _ _ + U
5. _ _ _ _ _ _

SOLUTIONS:

#89
1. RED + I
2. DIRE or RIDE
3. DRIED
4. BIDDER
5. BRAIDED

#90
1. FAN + L
2. FLAN
3. FINAL
4. FINALE
5. LEAFING

#91
1. ICE + L
2. LICE
3. SLICE
4. SPLICE
5. SPECIAL

#92
1. RUE + N
2. RUNE
3. RERUN
4. RETURN
5. NURTURE

#93

    1. LED + U
    2. _ _ _ _ + E
    3. _ _ _ _ _ + X
    4. _ _ _ _ _ _ + C
    5. _ _ _ _ _ _ _

#94

    1. LOW + Y
    2. _ _ _ _ + L
    3. _ _ _ _ _ + E
    4. _ _ _ _ _ _ + Y
    5. _ _ _ _ _ _ _

#95

    1. ERA + T
    2. _ _ _ _ + P
    3. _ _ _ _ _ + E
    4. _ _ _ _ _ _ + Z
    5. _ _ _ _ _ _ _

#96

Here's this section's last hidden letter puzzle which may be particularly challenging because it's a *double* hidden letter puzzle!

    1. ALL + C
    2. _ _ _ _ + _
    3. _ _ _ _ _ + _
    4. _ _ _ _ _ _ + T
    5. _ _ _ _ _ _ _

SOLUTIONS:

#93
1. LED + U
2. DUEL
3. ELUDE
4. DELUXE
5. EXCLUDE

#94
1. LOW + Y
2. OWLY
3. LOWLY
4. YELLOW
5. YELLOWY

#95
1. ERA + T
2. TEAR or RATE
3. PATER or TAPER
4. REPEAT
5. TRAPEZE

#96
1. ALL + C
2. CALL First hidden letter is: O
3. LOCAL Second hidden letter is: E
4. LOCALE
5. COLLATE

#97

    1. RAT + Y
    2. _ _ _ _ + S
    3. _ _ _ _ _ + A
    4. _ _ _ _ _ _ + H
    5. _ _ _ _ _ _ _

#98

    1. MAN + O
    2. _ _ _ _ + D
    3. _ _ _ _ _ + R
    4. _ _ _ _ _ _ + T
    5. _ _ _ _ _ _ _

#99

    1. RUE + P
    2. _ _ _ _ + T
    3. _ _ _ _ _ + E
    4. _ _ _ _ _ _ + D
    5. _ _ _ _ _ _ _

#100

    1. ONE + L
    2. _ _ _ _ + M
    3. _ _ _ _ _ + T
    4. _ _ _ _ _ _ + H
    5. _ _ _ _ _ _ _

SOLUTIONS:

#97
1. RAT + Y
2. TRAY
3. STRAY
4. ASTRAY
5. ASHTRAY

#98
1. MAN + O
2. MOAN
3. NOMAD or MONAD*
4. RANDOM
5. DORMANT or MORDANT**

*MONAD is a philosophical term meaning a unit of being such as a human, a deity, and others. There's one more philosophical term later on.

**DORMANT means "inactive", e.g. a volcano. MORDANT means having a biting or acidic manner. Keep these words in mind for the next two puzzles.

#99
1. RUE + P
2. PURE
3. ERUPT
4. REPUTE
5. ERUPTED

#100
1. ONE + L
2. LONE
3. LEMON or MELON*
4. MOLTEN**
5. MENTHOL

*LEMON, MELON. Here's the other pair of anagrams that are both the names of foods! Keep these words in mind for the next puzzle.

**MOLTEN. Did you remember to keep in mind the words from two puzzles ago? Did that puzzle's DORMANT, as in a volcano, and last puzzle's ERUPTED help you get this puzzle's MOLTEN, as in lava?!

VIII. 8-LETTER EXPANAGRAMS

#101
1. GEM + R
2. _ _ _ _ + E
3. _ _ _ _ _ + I
4. _ _ _ _ _ _ + N
5. _ _ _ _ _ _ _ + U
6. _ _ _ _ _ _ _ _

#102
1. LIP + E
2. _ _ _ _ + D
3. _ _ _ _ _ + S
4. _ _ _ _ _ _ + N
5. _ _ _ _ _ _ _ + D
6. _ _ _ _ _ _ _ _

#103
1. RUG + E
2. _ _ _ _ + S
3. _ _ _ _ _ + O
4. _ _ _ _ _ _ + N
5. _ _ _ _ _ _ _ + E
6. _ _ _ _ _ _ _ _

#104
1. TEE + R
2. _ _ _ _ + C
3. _ _ _ _ _ + I
4. _ _ _ _ _ _ + O
5. _ _ _ _ _ _ _ + S
6. _ _ _ _ _ _ _ _

71

SOLUTIONS:

#101
1. GEM + R
2. GERM
3. MERGE
4. REGIME or ÉMIGRÉ
5. REGIMEN
6. MERINGUE*

*This puzzle may not have been as easy as pie. Speaking of pie, did you remember to keep in mind the food words from the last puzzle? Did last puzzle's LEMON help you get this puzzle's MERINGUE, as in lemon meringue pie?!

#103
1. RUG + E
2. URGE
3. SURGE
4. ROGUES or GROUSE
5. SURGEON
6. GENEROUS

#104
1. TEE + R
2. TREE
3. ERECT
4. RECITE
5. COTERIE
6. ESOTERIC

The hidden letter puzzles in this section may be particularly challenging. As a result, there will be hints provided. Unlike the previous sections' hidden letter puzzles which were at the bottom of a page, this section's hidden letter puzzles will be designated as such and will appear at the top of a page. This is because the hints will be at the bottom. Hence, when you see the hidden letter puzzle designation at the top, please avert your eyes from the bottom of that page until you've had a crack at the puzzle! As a suggestion, please attempt the puzzle without the hint at first. Should you be stumped, go to the hint which will lead you to the hidden letter. Then insert the hidden letter in its blank and approach the puzzle as you normally would—but even then, the puzzle may still be challenging! Here's the first one in this section:

*Hidden Letter Puzzle:

#105
1. SIP + D
2. _ _ _ _ + E
3. _ _ _ _ _ + _
4. _ _ _ _ _ _ + R
5. _ _ _ _ _ _ _ + I
6. _ _ _ _ _ _ _ _

*Hidden Letter Hint: the hidden letter for Puzzle #105 is the third letter of the given word on the first line of Puzzle #1.

SOLUTIONS:

#105
1. SIP + D
2. DIPS
3. SPIED Hidden letter is: T
4. SPITED
5. STRIPED
6. SPIRITED

#106

    1. KIT + C

    2. _ _ _ _ + R

    3. _ _ _ _ _ + Y

    4. _ _ _ _ _ _ + E

    5. _ _ _ _ _ _ _ + R

    6. _ _ _ _ _ _ _

#107

    1. WET + H

    2. _ _ _ _ + I

    3. _ _ _ _ _ + R

    4. _ _ _ _ _ _ + D

    5. _ _ _ _ _ _ _ + E

    6. _ _ _ _ _ _ _

#108

    1. RIB + D

    2. _ _ _ _ + E

    3. _ _ _ _ _ + L

    4. _ _ _ _ _ _ + B

    5. _ _ _ _ _ _ _ + U

    6. _ _ _ _ _ _ _

SOLUTIONS:

#106
1. KIT + C
2. TICK
3. TRICK
4. TRICKY
5. RICKETY
6. TRICKERY

#107
1. WET + H
2. WHET
3. WHITE
4. WHITER or WITHER
5. WRITHED
6. WITHERED

#108
1. RIB + D
2. BIRD
3. BRIDE
4. BRIDLE
5. DRIBBLE
6. BLUEBIRD

*Hidden Letter Puzzle:

#109
   1. IRE + D
   2. _ _ _ _ + D
   3. _ _ _ _ _ + _
   4. _ _ _ _ _ _ + A
   5. _ _ _ _ _ _ _ + L
   6. _ _ _ _ _ _ _ _

#110
   1. BOO + E
   2. _ _ _ _ + D
   3. _ _ _ _ _ + M
   4. _ _ _ _ _ _ + R
   5. _ _ _ _ _ _ _ + S
   6. _ _ _ _ _ _ _

#111
   1. HAT + H
   2. _ _ _ _ + E
   3. _ _ _ _ _ + S
   4. _ _ _ _ _ _ + C
   5. _ _ _ _ _ _ _ + E
   6. _ _ _ _ _ _ _

#112
   1. OUR + S
   2. _ _ _ _ + C
   3. _ _ _ _ _ + C
   4. _ _ _ _ _ _ + S
   5. _ _ _ _ _ _ _ + W
   6. _ _ _ _ _ _ _

*Hidden Letter Hint: the hidden letter for Puzzle #109 is the second letter of the given word on the first line of Puzzle #1.

SOLUTIONS:

#109
1. IRE + D
2. DIRE or RIDE
3. DRIED Hidden letter is: E
4. DERIDE
5. READIED
6. DEADLIER

#110
1. BOO + E
2. OBOE
3. BOOED
4. BOOMED
5. BOREDOM
6. BEDROOMS

#111
1. HAT + H
2. HATH
3. HEATH
4. SHEATH
5. HATCHES
6. CHEETAHS

#112
1. OUR + S
2. SOUR
3. SCOUR
4. OCCURS
5. SUCCORS
6. CROWCUSS

#113

   1. HER + I

   2. _ _ _ _ + T

   3. _ _ _ _ _ + E

   4. _ _ _ _ _ _ + N

   5. _ _ _ _ _ _ _ + T

   6. _ _ _ _ _ _ _

#114

   1. LAB + E

   2. _ _ _ _ + T

   3. _ _ _ _ _ + D

   4. _ _ _ _ _ _ + O

   5. _ _ _ _ _ _ _ + D

   6. _ _ _ _ _ _ _

#115

   1. RED + B

   2. _ _ _ _ + I

   3. _ _ _ _ _ + S

   4. _ _ _ _ _ _ + U

   5. _ _ _ _ _ _ _ + S

   6. _ _ _ _ _ _ _

#116

   1. LIE + B

   2. _ _ _ _ + L

   3. _ _ _ _ _ + A

   4. _ _ _ _ _ _ + R

   5. _ _ _ _ _ _ _ + E

   6. _ _ _ _ _ _ _

SOLUTIONS:

#113
1. HER + I
2. HIRE or HEIR
3. THEIR
4. EITHER
5. THEREIN or NEITHER
6. THIRTEEN*

*THIRTEEN. Hope you're not too spooked or jinxed by this word, or *number,* that is! It's appropriate for Puzzle #113, in any case! While the number 13 has been traditionally deemed unlucky, the number seven, on the other hand, is deemed a lucky number. SEVEN has an anagram, EVENS, as in odds and evens. But seven is not an even number, which makes all this seem quite...*odd*!

#114
1. LAB + E
2. ABLE or BALE
3. BLEAT
4. TABLED
5. BLOATED
6. DEBTLOAD

#115
1. RED + B
2. BRED
3. BRIDE
4. DEBRIS
5. BRUISED
6. DISBURSE

#116
1. LIE + B
2. BILE
3. LIBEL
4. LIABLE
5. BRAILLE
6. RELIABLE

*Hidden Letter Puzzle:

#117
    1. RID + B
    2. _ _ _ _ + E
    3. _ _ _ _ _ + _
    4. _ _ _ _ _ _ + A
    5. _ _ _ _ _ _ _ + D
    6. _ _ _ _ _ _ _ _

#118
    1. ELM + O
    2. _ _ _ _ + D
    3. _ _ _ _ _ + S
    4. _ _ _ _ _ _ + R
    5. _ _ _ _ _ _ _ + E
    6. _ _ _ _ _ _ _

#119
    1. HAS + C
    2. _ _ _ _ + M
    3. _ _ _ _ _ + O
    4. _ _ _ _ _ _ + I
    5. _ _ _ _ _ _ _ + M
    6. _ _ _ _ _ _ _

#120
    1. RUE + P
    2. _ _ _ _ + S
    3. _ _ _ _ _ + S
    4. _ _ _ _ _ _ + P
    5. _ _ _ _ _ _ _ + S
    6. _ _ _ _ _ _ _ _

*Hidden Letter Hint: the hidden letter for Puzzle #117 is the third letter
of the given word on the first line of Puzzle #5.

81

SOLUTIONS:

#117
1. RID + B
2. BIRD
3. BRIDE Hidden letter is: G
4. BRIDGE
5. BRIGADE
6. ABRIDGED

#118
1. ELM + O
2. MOLE
3. MODEL
4. SELDOM
5. SMOLDER
6. REMODELS

#119
1. HAS + C
2. CASH
3. CHASM
4. MOCHAS
5. CHAMOIS
6. MACHISMO

#120
1. RUE + P
2. PURE
3. SUPER
4. PURSES
5. SUPPERS
6. SUPPRESS

#121

    1. GET + A
    2. _ _ _ _ + N
    3. _ _ _ _ _ + E
    4. _ _ _ _ _ _ + L
    5. _ _ _ _ _ _ _ + N
    6. _ _ _ _ _ _ _

#122

    1. PER + S
    2. _ _ _ _ + S
    3. _ _ _ _ _ + I
    4. _ _ _ _ _ _ + M
    5. _ _ _ _ _ _ _ + O
    6. _ _ _ _ _ _ _

#123

    1. SHE + R
    2. _ _ _ _ + I
    3. _ _ _ _ _ + C
    4. _ _ _ _ _ _ + B
    5. _ _ _ _ _ _ _ + M
    6. _ _ _ _ _ _ _

SOLUTIONS:

#121

1. GET + A
2. GATE
3. AGENT
4. NEGATE
5. ELEGANT
6. ENTANGLE

#122

1. PER + S
2. REPS
3. PRESS
4. SPIRES
5. IMPRESS or SIMPERS or PREMISS*
6. PROMISES

*PREMISS. No, that's not a typo. As an alternative spelling to the more familiar PREMISE, PREMISS is utilized, especially in logical philosophy, to mean a previous statement from which a conclusion is reached. PREMISE is more frequently employed to mean the essential situation in a book, film, and others. And PREMISES means the operating area or the building for a business.

Here's an example utilizing all three words: As it's a logical PREMISS that there are people who enjoy words, then word puzzles make an excellent PREMISE for a book, which those people could find on the PREMISES of a bookstore!

#123

1. SHE + R
2. HERS
3. HIRES or HEIRS
4. RICHES
5. BIRCHES
6. BESMIRCH

#124
1. ART + T
2. _ _ _ _ + E
3. _ _ _ _ _ + S
4. _ _ _ _ _ _ + G
5. _ _ _ _ _ _ _ + Y
6. _ _ _ _ _ _ _

#125
1. VIE + C
2. _ _ _ _ + O
3. _ _ _ _ _ + N
4. _ _ _ _ _ _ + N
5. _ _ _ _ _ _ _ + C
6. _ _ _ _ _ _ _

#126
1. CAN + L
2. _ _ _ _ + A
3. _ _ _ _ _ + R
4. _ _ _ _ _ _ + I
5. _ _ _ _ _ _ _ + V
6. _ _ _ _ _ _ _

#127
1. SEE + N
2. _ _ _ _ + U
3. _ _ _ _ _ + R
4. _ _ _ _ _ _ + D
5. _ _ _ _ _ _ _ + T
6. _ _ _ _ _ _ _

#128
1. ICE + P
2. _ _ _ _ + E
3. _ _ _ _ _ + R
4. _ _ _ _ _ _ + T
5. _ _ _ _ _ _ _ + D
6. _ _ _ _ _ _ _

SOLUTIONS:

#124
    1. ART + T
    2. TART
    3. TREAT
    4. TASTER
    5. TARGETS
    6. STRATEGY

#125
    1. VIE + C
    2. VICE
    3. VOICE
    4. NOVICE
    5. CONNIVE
    6. CONVINCE

#126
    1. CAN + L
    2. CLAN
    3. CANAL
    4. CARNAL
    5. CRANIAL
    6. CARNIVAL

#127
    1. SEE + N
    2. SEEN
    3. ENSUE
    4. ENSURE
    5. ENDURES
    6. DENTURES

#128
    1. ICE + P
    2. EPIC
    3. PIECE
    4. RECIPE or PIERCE
    5. RECEIPT
    6. DECREPIT

IX. 9-LETTER EXPANAGRAMS

#129

   1. RED + N
   2. _ _ _ _ + T
   3. _ _ _ _ _ + I
   4. _ _ _ _ _ _ + T
   5. _ _ _ _ _ _ _ + S
   6. _ _ _ _ _ _ _ _ + Y
   7. _ _ _ _ _ _ _ _

#130

   1. CAN + L
   2. _ _ _ _ + E
   3. _ _ _ _ _ + G
   4. _ _ _ _ _ _ + I
   5. _ _ _ _ _ _ _ + R
   6. _ _ _ _ _ _ _ _ + D
   7. _ _ _ _ _ _ _ _

#131

   1. ARE + M
   2. _ _ _ _ + D
   3. _ _ _ _ _ + E
   4. _ _ _ _ _ _ + N
   5. _ _ _ _ _ _ _ + O
   6. _ _ _ _ _ _ _ _ + P
   7. _ _ _ _ _ _ _ _

SOLUTIONS:

#129
1. RED + N
2. REND
3. TREND
4. TINDER
5. TRIDENT
6. STRIDENT
7. DENTISTRY

#130
1. CAN + L
2. CLAN
3. CLEAN or LANCE
4. GLANCE
5. ANGELIC
6. CLEARING
7. DECLARING

#131
1. ARE* + M
2. MARE or REAM
3. DREAM* or ARMED*
4. REMADE
5. MEANDER or RENAMED
6. ENAMORED* or DEMEANOR
7. PROMENADE

*If I may, I'd like to take the words from this puzzle to leave you with a few kind words of experience. These words have served me well relating to my passion for writing and words and creativity, and I hope these words may serve you well, too: Don't MEANDER if you're ENAMORED of something and ARE ARMED with a DREAM!

#132
1. EAR + R
2. _ _ _ _ + S
3. _ _ _ _ _ + E
4. _ _ _ _ _ _ + C
5. _ _ _ _ _ _ _ + T
6. _ _ _ _ _ _ _ _ + E
7. _ _ _ _ _ _ _ _ _

#133
1. AID + R
2. _ _ _ _ + S
3. _ _ _ _ _ + O
4. _ _ _ _ _ _ + E
5. _ _ _ _ _ _ _ + D
6. _ _ _ _ _ _ _ _ + B
7. _ _ _ _ _ _ _ _ _

#134
1. SEE + T
2. _ _ _ _ + A
3. _ _ _ _ _ + R
4. _ _ _ _ _ _ + T
5. _ _ _ _ _ _ _ + R
6. _ _ _ _ _ _ _ _ + C
7. _ _ _ _ _ _ _ _ _

SOLUTIONS:

#132
1. EAR + R
2. RARE
3. REARS
4. ERASER
5. CAREERS
6. CATERERS or RETRACES
7. RECREATES

#133
1. AID + R
2. ARID
3. RAIDS
4. RADIOS
5. ROADIES
6. ROADSIDE
7. BROADSIDE or SIDEBOARD

#134
1. SEE + T
2. TEES
3. TEASE
4. TEASER or EATERS
5. RESTATE
6. RETREATS
7. STREETCAR

#135

   1. ERE + T
   2. _ _ _ _ + A
   3. _ _ _ _ _ + C
   4. _ _ _ _ _ _ + N
   5. _ _ _ _ _ _ _ + N
   6. _ _ _ _ _ _ _ _ + I
   7. _ _ _ _ _ _ _ _

#136

   1. COP + E
   2. _ _ _ _ + U
   3. _ _ _ _ _ + R
   4. _ _ _ _ _ _ + R
   5. _ _ _ _ _ _ _ + D
   6. _ _ _ _ _ _ _ _ + E
   7. _ _ _ _ _ _ _ _

#137

   1. SIR + T
   2. _ _ _ _ + H
   3. _ _ _ _ _ + E
   4. _ _ _ _ _ _ + L
   5. _ _ _ _ _ _ _ + W
   6. _ _ _ _ _ _ _ _ + E
   7. _ _ _ _ _ _ _ _

SOLUTIONS:

#135
1. ERE + T
2. TREE
3. EATER
4. CREATE
5. REENACT
6. ENTRANCE
7. NECTARINE

#136
1. COP + E
2. COPE
3. COUPE
4. RECOUP
5. PROCURE
6. PRODUCER
7. PROCEDURE

#137
1. SIR + T
2. STIR
3. SHIRT
4. THEIRS
5. SLITHER
6. WHISTLER
7. ERSTWHILE

X.   10-LETTER EXPANAGRAMS

#138
1. SIN + E
2. _ _ _ _ + G
3. _ _ _ _ _ + N
4. _ _ _ _ _ _ + T
5. _ _ _ _ _ _ _ + L
6. _ _ _ _ _ _ _ _ + I
7. _ _ _ _ _ _ _ _ _ + G
8. _ _ _ _ _ _ _ _ _ _

#139
1. SIP + R
2. _ _ _ _ + M
3. _ _ _ _ _ + E
4. _ _ _ _ _ _ + O
5. _ _ _ _ _ _ _ + V
6. _ _ _ _ _ _ _ _ + I
7. _ _ _ _ _ _ _ _ _ + U
8. _ _ _ _ _ _ _ _ _ _

#140
1. AGE + M
2. _ _ _ _ + I
3. _ _ _ _ _ + N
4. _ _ _ _ _ _ + I
5. _ _ _ _ _ _ _ + R
6. _ _ _ _ _ _ _ _ + L
7. _ _ _ _ _ _ _ _ _ + C
8. _ _ _ _ _ _ _ _ _ _

SOLUTIONS:

#138
1. SIN + E
2. SINE
3. SINGE
4. ENSIGN
5. TENSING or NESTING
6. NESTLING
7. LISTENING or ENLISTING
8. GLISTENING

#139
1. SIP + R
2. RIPS
3. PRISM
4. PRIMES or SIMPER
5. PROMISE
6. IMPROVES
7. IMPROVISE
8. IMPERVIOUS

#140
1. AGE + M
2. GAME
3. IMAGE
4. ENIGMA
5. IMAGINE
6. MIGRAINE
7. REMAILING
8. RECLAIMING